SUPERNATIONALISTIC INTEGRATION:

THE EUROPEAN UNION

DISCUSSIONS IN EUROPEAN POLITICS

HUNTER L. KOCH I

IN COORDINATION WITH CURRICULUM FOR:

PS390 – EUROPEAN POLITICS

SAGINAW VALLEY STATE UNIVERSITY

UNIVERSITY CENTER, MICHIGAN

Table of Contents

A "UNITED EUROPE"

Europe has substantially evolved from a group of warring factions into a tightened alliance of a "united Europe". However, this process did not occur overnight, but rather through a long evolution through the last half of the twentieth, and now the twenty-first centuries.

After the mass chaos of the first half of the twentieth century and the failed efforts to thwart of future wars prior to World War II, ended in catastrophe (World War II), leaving Europe devastated. According to Gordon, had Europe unified around 1870, it would be the most productive place on earth today, but it fell into "chaos and economic devastation" as a result of conflict. (Gordon[1]) In 1949, the North Atlantic

---

[1] Gordon, Robert J. Two Centuries of Economic Growth: Europe Chasing the American Frontier. Cambridge: *National Bureau of Economic Research, Inc*, 2004. *ProQuest.* Web. 8 July 2015.

Treaty Organization (NATO), created the first supranational defense mechanism by Western Nations to defend against the Soviet threat, and thus lead the way for supranational organization in Europe.

European integration began in the European Steel and Coal Community, and eventually the European Economic Community (EEC), in uncharted waters. According to Patel, European history has been "patchy and fragile" prior to the Maastricht Treaty and the Single European Act came into effect during the 1980's. Those documents however played a large role in developing the Europe as we are able to see it today, making it a "potent and recognized force". Throughout the early stages of the Cold War, Europe as integrating the EEC was saw more as "peace and prosperity", while the latter stages showed the true goal of a "united Europe". (Patel[2])

The European Union (EU) as it was known after the Maastricht Treaty sat at the status quo deepening its integration though the end of the twentieth century. However, at the turn of the century, the Euro changed the game. According to Scharrer, the Euro's monetary unity before it was introduced into circulation created a united economy; yet, when people across Europe first saw the same currency in their own hands, people could see a "united Europe". Visibility of the tangible cash in the hands of about 300 million

---

[2] Patel, Kiran Klaus. "Provincialising European Union: Co-Operation and Integration in Europe in a Historical Perspective." *Contemporary European History* 22.4 (2013): 649-73. *ProQuest.* Web. 8 July 2015.

Europeans strongly raised its acceptance in the public eye. (Scharrer[3])

Accession of Eastern European states in 2004 dramatically changed the landscape of the EU. The EU had been dominated by the states of Western Europe for its entire history. Following the collapse of the Soviet state, and thus is puppeteering of Eastern Europe, those same nations were able to thoroughly integrate with the West for the first time in over 60 years. As displayed by Dangerfield, cooperation by the new democracies of Eastern Europe with the Trans-Atlantic community is vital to world economic integration. Whereas without, struggle and tension with the Russian juggernaut could continue. (Dangerfield[4]) Later in 2007, Romania

---

[3] Scharrer, Hans-Eckart. "From the Virtual to the Tangible Euro." *Intereconomics* 36.6 (2001): 277-8. *ProQuest.* Web. 8 July 2015.

[4] Dangerfield, Martin. "V4: A New Brand for Europe? Ten Years of Post-Accession Regional Cooperation in Central Europe."

and Bulgaria, and in 2013, Croatia, followed the same integration concepts in their accession. Europe as a whole was finally able to be considered "united".

Finally, the Treaty of Lisbon's creation of a bicameral legislative system with a stronger European Parliament united all Europeans equally in one single legislative body directly elected by the people. According to Church, the Treaty of Lisbon makes the citizen's role in the EU far greater, and at the same time makes parliament more responsible to the citizens. Also, the treaty creates a "new and stronger union". (Church[5]) Thus, the Treaty of Lisbon quickly and

The Poznan University of Economics Review 14.4 (2014): 71-90. _ProQuest._ Web. 8 July 2015.

[5] Church, Clive H., and David Phinnemore. "Understanding the Treaty of Lisbon." _Romanian Journal of European Affairs_ 10.2 (2010): 5-29. _ProQuest._ Web. 8 July 2015.

swiftly created the closest representation we can know to a "united Europe"

As shown within the Module One Lecture by French, the theory of integration has two theories within it. The first, neofunctionalism, explains the gradual increase in unity among the EU states. The EEC was a simple economic union, while through Maastricht and Lisbon, the European Union became so integrated that it eventually fell into a political union. The second, spillover, refers to the interconnectivity of economies and states in general causing each state to integrate and become more so integrated, in which political bodies attempt to influence the entire supranational authority rather than individual states. (French[6])

---

[6] French, Stewart. "PS 390 European Politics Module One Lecture." 9 July 2015. Lecture.

Specifically, the history of France in the European Union is one of utmost significance. France, one of the most ravaged nations during World War II, became a "charter member" of the origins of the European Union. Through efforts in NATO, the Marshall Plan, and others, France was rebuilt and became a dominant European power yet once again. The first major action by the French was Charles de Gaulle's veto in 1963 of the entry of the United Kingdom due to raw tenacity. At the same time France remained quite independent, tied in their own colonial military conflicts, including Vietnam. In 1992, France nearly voted no on the referendum to approve the Treaty of Maastricht, signaling a warning to European integrators. However, France began to deeply integrate thereafter with adopting the Euro at its inception. France's close deepening ties with NATO and other large world wide powers deepening has made France into a vital player in the EU.

Overall, integration in Europe has come at a gradual pace over time, but has become a vital part of world politics in general. Supranational organizations around the world have attempted to model the overall success of the EU, however have not been able to come close to the advanced standards which the EU incorporates. Integration across Europe has truly created a "united Europe"

There are multiple underlying reasons for the upcoming referendum in Britain over membership in the European Union. The House of Commons overwhelmingly supported the referendum as being the first time the current generation has had an in or out vote of whether to remain in the European Union or not. First of all, the United Kingdom has had a long history of referendums, from the recent Scottish Independence referendum to the other devolution, economic, and electoral referendums that are brought up in the article. Secondly, the

United Kingdom has had an historical resentment toward supernationalism and giving up its sovereignty. For example, the United Kingdom has not adopted the Euro as its currency, as well as the collective reluctance. Remnants of tensions between the Scottish National Party and other parties in British Government also are causing underlying tension on this issue.

Additionally, the late entrance of Britain in to the European Union, and the tension involved in that entry, have created a lasting impact on the attitude of the British people on the European Union today; while at the same time, devolutionary pressures are created by the long ago events at the time of the Union Acts. Overall, this is caused by the longstanding modern British culture. This has created overwhelming sense of regional identity and national identity, carrying over from the era of Margret Thatcher. Thus, with another Conservative victory in the 2015 general election, Prime Minister David Cameron promised this election, to what is a political move to gain more support rather than a vote for the people. However, the Labour Party also supported a referendum in the election. Likewise, on May 27th, the queen made a speech which addressed the referendum as she showed support for keeping the United Kingdom in the European Union.

The British people are seemingly skeptical of losing their identity and sovereignty, thus formulating reasoning that this referendum exist. Polling has showed support for withdrawal from the European Union to be at a high in 2014, significantly increasing from 2012 polling. At the same time however, the polls showed the public to have a more positive look on remaining in the European Union with a renegotiation of terms.

Perhaps the most complexing issue in this referendum is that it shows a divisive turn from partisan politics which have also ravaged trust in the British Government over the past years. Many officials from both major parties (Labour and Conservative) stand on either sides to affirm to or withdrawal from the European Union. Many economic and business entities in the European Union or around the world, are warming Britain of negative economic impacts in the case of a withdrawal.

Albeit, Euroscepticism is a major issue across Britain and the European Union abroad and will continue to cause turmoil across Europe. Certainly, Britain will have a difficult choice in this referendum, although, Prime Minster Cameron should not have much difficulty keeping Britain in the European Union.

Being the smallest state in the European Union (EU), Luxembourg is one of the few nations in Europe to have seen substantial benefit from joining. Thus, the most important event in the history of Luxembourg has been the signing of the

Treaty of Rome in 1957, and beginning the European Economic Community (EEC), for two very large reasons.

First, Luxembourg is an extremely small state, with a very small population, which also is landlocked. Traditionally, a nation such as this would be essentially powerless. However through originally Benelux, and more so through the EEC, Luxembourg's relative power has been inflated greatly. Although Luxembourg never used the veto power such as Charles de Gaulle and France used against the United Kingdom's accession, they still had the same power within the EEC as much larger France and Germany at the time. Even though Luxembourg's relative power diminished as reforms occurred within the EEC and the EU, Luxembourg remained a charter member, and thus, the original principles of the EU today are swayed to favor Luxembourg and the other charter members.

Secondly, and perhaps most recognizable to Luxembourg is the incredible amount of wealth. Luxembourg has the highest Gross Domestic Product (GDP) per capita in the World according to the International Monetary Fund's (IMF) 2014 estimates, equating to almost 112.000 United States Dollars (USD) per person. This far trumps Norway, which is second on the list at just over 97,000 USD per capita. Luxembourg's GDP per capita has increased by over three fold since 1960.

There is no doubt that the economic success that Luxembourg has had within the EU and the Eurozone, has helped a small, landlocked nation reach a level of worldwide influence that is extremely abnormal. Thus, Luxembourg's involvement in signing the Treaty of Rome and its charter membership, have made the Treaty of Rome the most important event in the history of modern Luxembourg.

Luxembourg's adoption of the Euro, and thus entrance into the Eurozone in 1999 has also greatly affected the nation's situation in Europe and the world. Luxembourg's GDP per capita since integrating the Euro has only increased by about 14 percent. However, an increase of population of about 27 percent over this 16 year period affects the meaning of that number greatly. Luxembourg's overall GDP has actually increased again by almost three fold since 1999.

However, today's growth of Luxembourg in the Eurozone is greatly different. Luxembourgish GDP has taken a major hit since the economic downturn greatly ravaged other nations such as Greece. Since 2008, Luxembourg's GDP has decreased by around nine percent, much more than the Eurozone average growth of around -2.9 percent.

These trends in Luxembourg can be compared with struggling economies. Greek GDP has dropped about 30 percent since 2008. Other small Eurozone states like Slovenia (GDP Growth ~-14%) have saw GDP fall much farther than the Eurozone average. Meanwhile, larger Eurozone states like France and Germany show moderate increases in GDP. And even struggling Italy shows below Eurozone average declines.

Although Luxembourg's position economically in the world has become larger since integrating the Euro, its striving economy has been slowed as a result of economic troubles elsewhere in the Eurozone. These issues across the Eurozone have hit small nations the hardest, and thus has recently turned the tide against Luxembourg's inflated presence in the European and World Community.

ORDER AND "PROCESS"

Within the European Union (EU), the process of "how a bill becomes a law" is woefully different then the simplicity of most national government. The European Union as a result of the Treaty of Lisbon now uses an "ordinary legislative procedure".

"Bills", originate as ideas from the European Commission. According to europa.eu, the official website of the European Union, the European Commission proposes new legislation after considering the impacts such legislation will have on the "economic, social, and environmental" factors of the EU. The Commission drafts as they call "impact assessments" which pinpoint pros and cons to the action which they are requesting. As the Commission does not have many advising opportunities, it seeks input from a multitude of organizations at the local, regional, and national level. The Commission's website even includes the ability for the public to contribute input. Likewise national parliaments are eligible to display any reservations if they believe the issue is "better handled at a national level than an EU level". (europa.eu[7])

Secondly comes the standard legislative procedure, where the new bicameral legislature takes action on a particular piece of legislation. European Parliament, a body of directly elected Members of European Parliament (MEP's) hold the lower house of the legislature while the upper house is held by the European Council, made up of representatives from each of the twenty-eight member states.

Again according to europa.eu, both the Council and the Parliament are eligible to make amendments to the legislation. Amendment

---

[7] "How EU Decisions Are Made." *EUROPA* -. N.p., n.d. Web. 09 July 2015.

recommendations are often made by the European Commission as well but must be formally acted upon by the two legislative bodies. When both houses are unable to agree on the amendments, the legislation is taken for a second reading. Parliament has the sole ability to "block legislation if it cannot agree with the Council". However, if amendments are agreed to, the legislation can be directly passed. (europa.eu[8])

According to the official website of the European Parliament, europarl.europa.eu, references Conciliation as being the last chance for amendments to be agreed on by both parties. Conciliation committees are made up of fifty-six members. Twenty-eight members come from the European Council, one from each member state. Twenty-eight other members come from European Parliament, where representation is based on the proportion of party/alliance control.

---

[8] "How EU Decisions Are Made." *EUROPA* -. N.p., n.d. Web. 09 July 2015.

Members of the committee attempt to create a joint text. If a text can be scribed and agreed on, the presidents of Parliament and Council sign off on it to become law. Whereas, when it cannot be agreed on, the legislation is dead. (europarl.europa.eu[9])

Albeit the process, the European Commission has the most influence on legislation in the European Union. According to Sideri, the European Commission is one of the more private bodies in all of politics. Even with efforts after Maastricht, transparency of the Commission is difficult to see. The "organizational culture" is one that is only "a system of political bargaining". (Sideri[10]) The relative private life that the

---

[9] "Conciliations and Codecision - CODE." *Conciliations and Codecision - CODE*. N.p., 20 Apr. 2004. Web. 09 July 2015.

[10] Sideri, Katerina. "The European Commission and the Law-Making Process: Compromise as a Category of Praxis." *International Journal of Law in Context* 1.2 (2005): 155-82. *ProQuest*. Web. 9 July 2015.

commission enjoys allows the body to discuss and maneuver policy in unconventional ways. Although this may be good or bad, it gives the Commission incredible power in the decision making process. As can be seen by Stormowska, Commission members, and even presidents refer to "internal coordination" as ex-president Barroso referenced to it. (Stormowska[11])

The European Commission's weak organizational structure may not be a coincidence though. According to Trondal, the system is structured so that the top of the Commission can "command" action. The Commission remains organized in special ways for the simplicity and purpose that does not get in the way of its function. The integration of the different parts of

---

[11] Stormowska, Marta. "The Normalization of the European Commission: Politics and Bureaucracy in the EU Executive/The European Commission of the Twenty-First Century." *The Polish Quarterly of International Affairs* 23.2 (2014): 127-31. *ProQuest.* Web. 9 July 2015.

the Commission allow executive duties of the Commission to be carried out. Although the Commission is intended to represent what is best for the whole of Europe, national and personal interests often create influences. Meanwhile, the Commission also is able to select their own officials rather than having to listen for mandates or appointments from the national governments. (Trondal[12]) The Commission is more or less a self-controlling body. Although other pieces of EU governance have been given more and more power, the Commission is still the most powerful force for EU ideology and legislative work.

The only minor, yet incredible power in the creation of legislation rests within the fifty-six members of the conciliation committees. According to Franchino and Mariotto, joint text formulated by the committee can get dragged

---

[12] Trondal, Jarle. "Contending Decision-Making Dynamics within the European Commission." *Comparative European Politics* 5.2 (2007): 158-78. *ProQuest.* Web. 9 July 2015.

more toward the original text of either Parliament or Council. Although there are weaknesses within the structure of Conciliation committees, the legislation can be "reconciled". Parliament and Council though have the power of conciliation vested in their hands rather than with the Commission (Franchino and Mariotto[13]). Although influence comes from the Commission, the committee has the final say and can virtually kill the Commission's dearest legislation.

Ultimately, the EU's system of "a bill becoming a law" is somewhat complicated and has many different routes which legislation can take to become law. Commission may control legislation, and almost exclusively the legislative agenda; yet, Parliament and the Council hold the

---

[13] Franchino, Fabio, and Camilla Mariotto. "Explaining Negotiations in the Conciliation Committee." *European Union politics* 14.3 (2013): 345-65. *ProQuest.* Web. 9 July 2015.

ability to make the final call, even if it is not exactly what they would like to do.

In the debate over European net neutrality the European Parliament had the strong, upper hand on controlling the legislative process. However, there was many different ways that this advantage was taken by Parliament.

Perhaps the most important part of Parliament's interaction with this policy is the big amendments that it passed to tag onto the law. Amendment 234 defined "net neutrality" as being "the principle according to which all internet traffic is treated equally", being a strong definition that mirrors the only two other strong net neutrality laws passed in Slovenia and the Netherlands prior to this act. Also, the definition of "specialized services" in Amendment 235 and strengthened in Amendment 236, drove home Parliament's influence and dominance over this act. Although many of the amendments to this were not passed by parliament, the strongest and most notable were.

Parliament also had a strategic upper hand in this discussion because this was a very public issue, which directly effects everyday people more so than other action. The European Parliament, in being directly elected by the people, is susceptible to pressures from lobbyists and interest groups.

As with all policy in the European Union, the origins of this act came from the European Commission; specifically, digital agenda chief, Neelie Kroes originated the efforts. Her efforts in this act brought in very public issues that hit the pocketbook of many Europeans. Thus, the original influence behind this act came from the European Commission, but was carried out and crafted by the European Parliament.

European Parliament's responsibility to the people drove the benefits of the act's most important elements. The creation of a more unified European media market would lower mobile phone costs when crossing "intra-European borders". Business also finds a benefit, especially small and "startup" businesses looking to become more pan-European. Net neutrality as proposed by Kroes, outlaws phone carriers stopping services on their networks which increase demand and profit in their own services.

However, specialized services remained a topic that net neutrality advocates wanted defined. Subsequently, Amendments 235 and 236 as passed by Parliament solved the issues raised by constituents. On this issue though, Kroes and the Commission were defeated. Leftist parties within Parliament rejoiced as did Kroes. Parliament was able to take the upper hand and use their public appeal and clout to drive home a somewhat controversial legislation in the manner that Parliament itself wanted.

Upon reading the amendments, it is evident that Parliament truly has an upper hand. The commission is only able to propose ideas once an action is under consideration. Parliament has the full ability to act as it did in this case. The council of ministers still needs to finalize the legislation before it becomes law. It is hard to deny action taken by the legislative body directly elected by the European people on an issue that directly effects many Europeans, especially after a 534-25 vote.

Activist groups have put the European Parliament in the situation that they are now, where MEP's are now forced to listen to the people rather than the European Telecommunications companies whom fear the legislations impact on their services. Wherefore, European Parliament has had a definite strong-hold on controlling and crafting European net neutrality legislation, and should continue to have greater power as Parliament racks in support from the people who elect them.

Perhaps the most important legislation passed by the European Union as a whole effects small nations such as Luxembourg most adversely. The interoperability of the trans-European rail system is the most important piece of legislation allowing for European infrastructure to accommodate the vast economic growth and integration that is desired.

From the Luxembourgish perspective, it is very simple. Luxembourg in being a small and landlocked nation requires a vast amount of over-land trade with neighboring nations. Steel exports make up around 29 percent of the total Luxembourgish exports, which often go to neighboring France and Belgium by rail. Belgium's top three import and export partners (Belgium, France, and Germany) require rail service. However, nations across Europe and around trade with Luxembourg routinely.

Albeit, Luxembourg is mainly a white-collar service industry nation. Tourism also plays a major role in society, welcoming almost one million visitors per year which rely on train service on many pan-European vacations. Agricultural exports, although small and regional, are strongly subsidized, with the main export being white wine, commonly consumed on a lesser scale in neighboring Germany, France, and Belgium, requiring rail transport.

Infrastructure is vital to any and all economies around the world. Luxembourg's reliance on rail service throughout Europe is large, and it's most important mean for transportation. Reliance on rail interoperability helps maintain Luxembourg's position within Europe.

On a more everyday citizen note, high speed passenger rail lines within the Benelux zone, and the interoperability and connectivity with French and German high speed lines allow for convenient travel for tourists and European residents.

European interoperability for rail service has made an incredible difference for Europe as a whole, but specifically for Luxembourg. Without acts such as this, Luxembourg would be more isolated and less interconnected with the world economically and fail to have the tourism revenues it brings in today. Rail service has been vaulted as the main transportation for Europe, and Luxembourg benefits more than the average for that interconnected service.

The European Union (EU) has a unique judicial process due to the complexity of being an international organization, rather than a unitary state. This structure comes from many struggles for autonomy and universal recognition, sharing and presiding over national constitutional courts, and according to Lenaerts, "the interlocking system of jurisdiction of the community courts" (Lenaerts[14]).

The European Court of Justice (ECJ), established in Luxembourg is the judicial wing of the European Union. The ECJ is responsible for interpreting EU law. National law is thus dealt with in national courts, unless, it interferes with EU primary or secondary law.

There is a two-step process for the operation of the ECJ. As described by europa.eu, the official website of the European Union, each case goes through a written and oral stage. First, in the written phase the case is assigned to a specific "judge-rapporteur" and an advocate general. Here both parties read the documents of the argument. The Court then meets to decide

---

[14] Lenaerts, Koen. "THE RULE OF LAW AND THE COHERENCE OF THE JUDICIAL SYSTEM OF THE EUROPEAN UNION." *Common Market Law Review* 44.6 (2007): 1625-59. *ProQuest.* Web. 27 July 2015.

the further steps of the case. If the case requires the "oral phase", what most would consider trial, the Court will provide specifications for said trial and determine the significance and need of an official opinion from the advocate general. The oral phase then allows lawyers to give their arguments and be asked questions by judges and the advocate general. If an official opinion of the advocate general is desired, said opinion is given after the hearing from which the verdict is made by the Court's justices (europa.eu[15]).

Since the development of the European Court of Justice, as referred to by Alter, it "is an unusually influential international court". Of which, the courts extreme autonomy has allowed it to decide cases against national interests in

---

[15] "Court of Justice of the European Union (CJEU)." *EUROPA*. N.p., n.d. Web. 27 July 2015. <http://europa.eu/about-eu/institutions-bodies/court-justice/index_en.htm>.

many cases (Alter[16]). The Court's relative autonomy and power has continuously been established and upheld through many major cases. In *Costa v ENEL (1964)*, the court ruled that law of the European Community was supreme over national law, and thus, gave the ECJ itself the power to determine such action (Costa v. ENEL[17]). Subsequently, this ruling was backed up to allow the ECJ to strike down provisions of national law conflicting EU law in *Amministrazione Delle Finanze Dello Stato v Simmenthal (1978)*.

Vaubel describes the ECJ as being the "engine of integration" within the European Union. The ECJ remains to be the most certain

---

[16] Alter, Karen J. "Who are the "Masters of the Treaty?": European Governments and the European Court of Justice." *International Organization* 52.1 (1998): 121-47. *ProQuest.* Web. 27 July 2015.

[17] Costa v ENEL. European Court of Justice. 3 June 1964. European Union, n.d. Web. 27 July 2015.

and definite centralizing feature of the EU, in being that it must remain centralized with its power to remain effective and legitimate. The ECJ remains not as just a "constitutional court" however. Similar to other federal-like nations, the Court of Justice remains tied into the laws of its subdivisions, similar to how the United States Supreme Court can rule on laws of the states. Centralization creates a "bias" within the Court to rule in the interest of supremacy (Vaubel[18]). This bias is what makes the ECJ an aid to furthering integration. For integration to occur, the power shift from national governments to the EU central authority must continue, centralizing institutions as the ECJ began far ago.

---

[18] Vaubel, Roland. "Constitutional Courts as Promoters of Political Centralization: Lessons for the European Court of Justice."*European Journal of Law and Economics* 28.3 (2009): 203-22. *ProQuest.* Web. 27 July 2015.

The ECJ has had considerable impacts on member states. Garrett summarizes the ECJ rulings to be similar to the United States Supreme Court as well. The court is creditable because of the early rulings giving the court great power. To the advantage of member states, their principles were somewhat intertwined in the makeup of the ECJ with legal integration. Member states no longer have the need to make rulings on treaties regarding the EU as well, allowing for rulings to be much quicker and more direct. The ECJ also gives national governments a platform to settle disputes between member states and/or the EU itself. On the other hand, the ECJ has devolutionized the sole autonomy of national courts. National law decisions made by the national courts are subject to further litigation before the ECJ, and thus, results in conflict as the ECJ sticks its hand in national politics (Garrett[19])

As concluded by Caldeira and Gibson, support for the ECJ by member states and their constituents grows with increased exposure to the court. Member states are more inclined to support the centrality of the ECJ, with it being that the knowledgeable public supports it as well. However, the low transparency that the Court has with the mainstream public remains an issue, and it is expected that the ECJ will need to make rulings that effect the mass public (Caldeira and Gibson[20]). Thus, member states are somewhat

---

[19] Garrett, Geoffrey, R. D. Kelemen, and Heiner Schulz. "The European Court of Justice, National Governments, and Legal Integration in the European Union." *International Organization* 52.1 (1998): 149-76. *ProQuest.* Web. 27 July 2015.

[20] Caldeira, Gregory A., and James L. Gibson. "The Legitimacy of the Court of Justice in the European Union: Models of Institutional Support." *The American Political Science Review* 89.2 (1995): 356. *ProQuest.* Web. 27 July 2015.

locked into the integration that the ECJ has created. Albeit, the benefits of the ECJ to the member states coincide with the positive public interest effect that the Court has created.

The complicated legal structure of the European Union and the European Court of Justice is a sign of future integration for Europe. This process is likely to change in the future as the EU continues to evolve, yet, the ECJ remains a desirable option for European regionalism.

The European Commission in being the most powerful executive and legislative authority in the European Union (EU) creates an imbalance in many executive duties, including investigations. These imbalances and fights over breaches of power between the Commission and business/citizens create drawn out cases such as the article provides over fishing policy. Albeit the 21st century reforms of the Commission's investigational powers, according to Varriale, the reforms simply appealed to the people and business without truly being "proactive" and complete the fix to the problems warranting the reform. (Varriale[21])

Dawn raids by the Commission against Deutsche Bahn in three German locations over the second quarter of 2011 sparked controversy over the authority and limits of the Commission in searches, more specifically over "fishing". The supranational Commission and Deutsche Bahn became litigants in the European Court of Justice (ECJ) as a result of the raids. The commission acting on behalf of all of Europe believed the wide scope of searches should be allowed, while from the side of a business litigant, Deutsche Bahn believed their investigation was illegal on multiple grounds. Deutsche Bahn believed that the

---

[21] Varriale, Gemma. "Why EC Antitrust Reforms are Merely Cosmetic." *International Financial Law Review* (2011) *ProQuest.* Web. 15 July 2015.

Commission failed to receive "judicial authorization" and the investigation had too broad of scope, which it subsequently obtained documents that were unwarranted.

Two steps to the process of the evolution in this case were extremely important. But, first, the General Courts had the weakest influence because of the additional appeal opportunities above that court. The general court denied all appeals, upholding the actions of the Commission due to "lack of proof" by Deutsche Bahn; yet, Deutsche Bahn was able to continue appeal to the ECJ for a decision from the Advocate-General.

Unlike, partisan Attorney General's in America, Advocate General's issue opinions on cases as an appointed wing of the ECJ itself. Although the Advocate General holds no definitive power, it is able to swing the tide of a case, opening up new viewpoints and discussion over the topics. Advocate General Wahl agreed that the commission did not require judicial approval. However, Wahl opened up new discussions on the remainder, citing violations of regulation 1/2003. Deutsche Bahn was never informed that the scope of the latter raids, were a response to the documents of the first.

Regardless of the Advocate General's decision, the ECJ still holds the muster and the heaviest clout in the EU judicial process. According to Bergkamp and Herbatschek, the ECJ must not take entire opinions as the truth, as could be saw in many cases overtime, especially when dealing with regulations, of which can create the largest of differentiated opinions. (Bergkamp and Herbatschek[22]). The final stand by the ECJ made a definitive ruling on

---

[22] Bergkamp, Lucas, and Nicolas Herbatschek. "The "Once an Article, always an Article" Approach: Reflections on the Advocate General's Opinion on the Concept of "Articles" Under REACH." *European Journal of Risk Regulation : EJRR* 6.1 (2015): 155-64. *ProQuest.* Web. 15 July 2015.

a variety of common topics. Since the ECJ is built on a woven combination of common and civil law, the precedence of this decision may have a continued and lasting impact as a result of judicial review.

The ECJ's most definitive answer of the appeal was the universal agreeance of all authorities that the Commission did not need judicial authorization from national courts to conduct these searches, hence citing safeguards in 1/2003. The ECJ was convinced though along with Advocate General Wahl and Deutsche Bahn, that the investigation must stay within the original scope, and information from such, must not be used for other purpose. The ECJ also claimed the "irregularity" of the first search caused the illegality of the second and third to be plausible.

The overwhelming clout over judicial process, and perhaps the entire European Union

Bureaucracy rests within the hands of the European Court of Justice. The ECJ in this case was able to pull back unequal power and reinforce regulation on the Commission, who still hold vast power, by requiring well defined scopes while balancing the Commissions ability to take action without the national courts. As can be seen in Esteve, the ECJ has a definitive role to play in the enforcement of community and European law, balancing the fine line of national versus supranational interests with direct effects. The ECJ, thus with its primary law, is able to fundamentally shift power across Europe with broad constitutional law. (Esteve[23])

The European Court of Justice (ECJ) has made a considerable amount of major rulings,

---

[23] Esteve, Joaquín Sarrión. "Constitutional Limits to European Integration in the New Member States After the Biggest Enlargement." *The Poznan University of Economics Review* 14.3 (2014): 58-72. *ProQuest.* Web. 15 July 2015.

particularly stemming from the Republic of Italy. However, perhaps the largest ruling in not just Italy, but the European Union (EU) as a whole is *Flaminio Costa v ENEL (1964)*. Costa owned shares in an electrical company in Italy and strongly opposed the nationalization of the electric companies in Italy. Costa argued that the actions were against the Treaty of Rome and the Constitution of Italy. Because the Treaty of Rome, from 1958, had held no supremacy over the Italian Electricity Nationalization Law of 1962, the Italian Constitutional Court ruled with "*lex posterior derogat legi anteriori/priori*" or that the subsequent law rules and upheld the Nationalization Law. The Italian Government dismissed need for an ECJ ruling.

The ECJ made a "half and half" ruling on the case. The ECJ ruled infavor of the Italian Government because decisions regarding Treaty of Rome violations against the government could only be pursued by the European Commission, as individuals have a lack of "direct effect" from the treaty's provisions. On the other hand, the ECJ ruled with Costa that an individual had the right to argue a matter of European Law before the national courts, as otherwise, review of such law would be ineffective. Thus, EU laws under the Treaty of Rome and subsequent EU treaties and laws hold supremacy over national law.

This case was a good event for Italy and other EU member states, even if it does not initially seem like it. Subsequent action in *Frontini v. Ministero delle Finanze (1974),* required national courts to enforce the supremacy of EU law in their own national courts, ruling the plaintiff in the case needed to wait for Italian Constitutional Court to make a ruling prior to taking action. Thus, *Costa v ENEL*, cleared up the long process of lengthy ECJ review over laws and allowed the national courts to take firm action when an ECJ ruling was of little to no use. Secondly, the national courts are given some autonomy with this decision, allowing them to make their own individual, case by case rulings in the absence of an ECJ decision.

More specifically, the ECJ with *Costa v ENEL* supported the policy of direct effect, that being national courts being directly responsible to enforce EU law and rights. *Van Gend en Loos v Nederlandse Administratie der Belastingen (1962),* first established that individuals could appeal to national courts for a breach of EU treaty provisions which citizens relied on.

Direct effect of EU provisions along with the supremacy of EU law has simplified and shortened the length of cases within the EU and member states. The ability for the Italian Constitutional Court to make decisions with autonomy, places the national court in a very advantageous and powerful position to make rulings saving the Italian Government from Commission intervention.

A BIGGER EU – EXPANSION POLITICS

The expansion of the European Union (EU) is one of great political conflict and of a multitude of economic, political, and social consequence. While previous accessions have been relatively innocent, the current European and world wide climate is one which allows debates over current candidate states.

The expansion process of the EU is a complicated multi-step process according to Article 49 of the Treaty on European Union. The article opens membership opportunities to all European nations. Applicant nations must meet EU requirements on an array of social and political issues of the democratic process. The European Commission, European Council, and European Parliament must approve the application before the process can begin. During application, the Commission reevaluates the country's political and economic standing as well as its ability to contribute as a member state and be able to adapt EU structure. If the candidate state meets "absorption capacity", accession negotiations begin. As the "cornerstone" of the adoption process, accession negotiations make certain the candidate is adaptable to EU law and meet "obligations as an EU member state". Once the all of the chapters, or topics, of the accession negotiations are completed, the accession treaty is begun. The Council begins the process after approval from Parliament and the Commission. Subsequently, the accession treaty is drafted with all of the detail from negotiations and the accession information. The treaty lastly must be ratified by all member states and the new member state before accession finally occurs (Treaty on European Union[24]).

The first accomplishment for EU expansion came with the accession of the United Kingdom,

---

[24] Treaty on European Union, § 49 (European Union 1993). Web.

one of the Western European power players along with counterparts Ireland and Denmark. Balmer, et al concludes that the United Kingdom is a very special situation. There are always devolutionary pressures which strain its EU relationship (Balmer, et al[25]). The United Kingdom's accession was strenuous though, as the French attempted to block it for years. Subsequently, the fit of an independently thinking nation like the United Kingdom in the EU, favors its ever present potential split. These 1973 enlargements greatly mirror the 1995 accessions for wealthy capitalist traditions in Sweden, Finland, and Austria.

Expansion in the Mediterranean saw an end to Military Rule in Spain, Portugal, and Greece. As Kay says precisely, Mediterranean expansion was to "secure democracy and promote economic development" in moderately powerful

---

[25] Bulmer, Simon, et al. "UK Devolution and the European Union: A Tale of Cooperative Asymmetry?" *Publius* 36.1 (2006): 75-93.*ProQuest.* Web. 1 Aug. 2015.

nations, of which was a grand success and built remarkable ties and development with Western Europe (Kay[26]).

The modern swath of EU expansion, included the former puppet states of the Soviet bloc plus some smaller outlying states. As Wesolowsky states, former Soviet puppet states saw the European Union as being a "ticket back" in to the modern developed world. Eastern Europe was saw as an investment ground for Western Europeans, just as West Germans invested in East Germany's reintegration in the 1990's. Eastern Europeans yearned for inclusion in their "rightful place" (Wesolowsky[27]). Eastern Europe achieved inclusion with the 2004 and

---

[26] Kay, John. "FT.Com Site : John Kay: The Right to Join Europe is Not a Reward." *FT.com* (2004): 1. *ProQuest.* Web. 1 Aug. 2015.

[27] Wesolowsky, Tony. "East Meets West: European Union Expansion and the Troubled Former Communist Countries." *Multinational Monitor* 23.5 (2002): 9-11. *ProQuest.* Web. 1 Aug. 2015.

2007 accessions. Later, Croatia, the former Yugoslav state achieved accession in 2013.

Issues surrounding further expansion are detailed in the Copenhagen Criteria. As cited by the European Commission's *Accession Criteria*, candidate nations must be politically fit, thus being a structured democracy and following democratic principles. Second, the candidate must be economically strong, and more so, stable, in the capitalist world. Last and most important, the candidate must be able to "hold its end of the bargain" as a member state; thus, this is assured only through proper and successful accession negotiations (European Commission[28]). The largest struggle for expansion is to find candidate countries that are able to meet the

---

[28] "Accession Criteria." *EU*. European Commission, n.d. Web. 01 Aug. 2015.
<http://ec.europa.eu/enlargement/policy/glossary/terms/accession-criteria_en.htm>.

Copenhagen Criteria, as well as fit to be geographically and culturally European.

Contrary to the Copenhagen Criteria, and recent addition and former Yugoslav state Croatia, Serbia remains an intriguing candidate to join the European Union. Asia News Monitor presents one of the few positive details to Serbian accession, in the cession of Kosovo. Serbia is the largest market in the former Yugoslavia, which could benefit the EU economically (Asia News Monitor); yet, Serbia faces strong challenges in its pursuit of EU membership.

International relations remain the cornerstone negative for Serbia's bid. Asia News Monitor also brings up two international conflicts for Serbia. First, Croatia, the newest EU accession, was a major wartime rival of the Yugoslav remnant Serbia in the breakup of Yugoslavia. Additionally, comparisons of post-Yugoslavian demise are brought up between success in EU members Croatia and Slovenia, shadowing Serbia. Second, Serbia's largest ally is the Russian juggernaut (Asia News Monitor[29]). Meanwhile, Cooley refers to the Serbia-Russia alliance as being "traditional" (Cooley[30]), as it stood since before World War I. Current EU states, particularly major defense players, will remain on edge to get full support of Serbia, which brings the Serb-Russian alliance back into play.

Although, the Kosovo issue is being resolved, the territorial integrity of neighbors remains a large issue for Serbian accession. Kosovo is recognized by 22 EU member states, who are unlikely to support Serbian accession

---

[29] "European Union/Serbia: EU Brokers Kosovo Deal, Opens Door to Serbia Accession." *Asia News Monitor* Apr 23 2013. *ProQuest.*Web. 1 Aug. 2015 .

[30] Cooley, Alexander. "Western Values as Power Politics: The Struggle for Mastery in Eurasia." *Global Dialogue* 11 (2009): 82-91.*ProQuest.* Web. 1 Aug. 2015.

without the recognition of Kosovo. Secondly, Serbian ties to Bosnian Serbs and the conflict of the Bosnian War further intensifies doubt that Serbia can fully integrate and fulfill its obligations in the European Union. Additionally, many EU and NATO joint members sent peacekeeping troops to fend off Serbian attacks in Bosnia just over 20 years ago.

Serbian accession into the European Union looks extremely unlikely over the foreseeable future. Serbia carries a significant amount of cultural baggage stemming from claims of genocide by Bosnia. The European Union's members will not be able to see Serbia as a politically stable environment, capable of producing a positive membership in the EU, and thus, Serbia's bid for EU membership is doomed.

The complicated and long process of EU expansion is one that allows a proper and delicate screening of candidates, securing the prosperity of the EU for the future. Thus, the newfound sense of controversy over future expansion is one of necessity and not one of bureaucratic mischief.

Among the list of nations with potential membership in the European Union (EU), the Former Yugoslav Republic of Macedonia (FYR Macedonia) remains one of the most intriguing. The chances for FYR Macedonia's membership remain somewhat strong, albeit major roadblocks remain.

The initial issue for FYR Macedonia's candidacy is relations with Greece. As Ivanovski best says, FYR Macedonia-Greek relations are substantively "one of those perverse, inherently unsolvable centuries-old problems dragging from one era to another in different forms and making things difficult for all the parties involved" as it is an issue more over honor and respect than real politics (Ivanovski[31]).

In real political issues, the BBC article "EU Enlargement: The next seven" points to the amount of progress that has been done within FYR Macedonia to become equitable for accession. Election conflicts in FYR Macedonia have been common although EU officials claim recent rounds to be more "transparent" (BBC[32]).

As stated from Maleska and Maleski, the withdrawal of Yugoslavian influence in 1991 left the nation vulnerable to political turmoil caused by ethnic division. The United Nations' defense mission to FYR Macedonia and the intrusions by European Community (EC) and North Atlantic

---

[31] Ivanovski, Hristijan. "The Macedonia-Greece dispute/difference Over the Name Issue: Mitigating the Inherently Unsolvable." *New Balkan Politics* 14 (2013): 1. *ProQuest.* Web. 30 July 2015.

[32] "EU Enlargement: The next Seven - BBC News." *BBC News.* British Broadcasting Corporation, 2 Sept. 2014. Web. 30 July 2015.

Treaty Organization (NATO) member Greece, left animosity in the region. Consistent Albanian nationalism threatened the new government, although the one issue all ethnic groups can agree on is European integration (Maleska and Maleski[33]).

On the other hand, Mitropolitski claims that ethnic tensions fuel nationalistic and far right-wing political organizations in FYR Macedonia as a fresh democracy. However, FYR Macedonia's government and citizens have a lack of stamina to participate in long-winded political discussions (Mitropolitski[34]).

---

[33] Maleska, Mirjana, and Denko Maleski. "Macedonia's Road to the European Union." *New Balkan Politics* 10 (2009): 1. *ProQuest.* Web. 30 July 2015.

[34] Mitropolitski, Simeon. "The Role of European Union Integration in Post-Communist Democratization in Bulgaria and Macedonia." *Canadian Slavonic Papers* 55.3 (2013): 365-VII. *ProQuest.* Web. 30 July 2015.

Although FYR Macedonia remains optimistic of its ability to join the EU and its integration, internal integration remains a necessary component. This situation was common in many of the Warsaw Pact nations that later joined the EU though. Fresh democracies need an exorbitant amount of guidance to raise to the standards which the EU sets forth.

Ironically, FYR Macedonia's bid for EU membership mirrors Greece's accession also. Both nations were/are coming out of militarized governments and likewise had complications upon application. Both nations economically were not similar. Greece's 1981 Gross Domestic Product (GDP) per capita sat just above 5,000 United States Dollars (USD), similar to FYR Macedonia's current GDP per capita of approximately 5,000 USD.

Tensions with other candidate nations remain an issue, particularly with Serbia. FYR

Macedonia as well as other former Yugoslav states are ahead of Serbia's push for EU accession. Also, Kosovo's independence struggle with Serbia is an issue on the FYR Macedonia-Serbia border, particularly as it relates to ethnic devolutionary pressures within FYR Macedonia.

However, as Sokolowska displays, the EU's big players remain very interested in solving the Balkan Crisis that has plagued Europe for decades. Germany particularly looks to exert control in the region economically (Sokolowska[35]). German influence in the Balkans show the big players in Europe do not see the western Balkans to be a particularly strong area, and moreover as an area subordinate to Western Europe and the

---

[35] Sokolowska, Patrycja. ""Soft Power" in the Promotion of Germany's Political and Economic Interests." *The Polish Quarterly of International Affairs* 22.2 (2013): 94-110. *ProQuest*. Web. 30 July 2015.

other territorial expansions for the EU into stronger and more stable nations.

While FYR Macedonia sees European integration as a positive for their own economies, other EU states are not quite as friendly to the opportunity. With the EU's accession for Slovenia and Croatia, both former Yugoslav states, members saw the cultural and economic differences to be manageable and relatively stable. Historical issues will hold up the process allowing for economic recovery for FYR Macedonia and other west Balkan candidate neighbors. Within the next decade membership for FYR Macedonia is very likely, although the nation must prove it can hold up on the world stage and find some way to cooperate with neighbors and the remainder of the EU. And likewise, FYR Macedonia will have to find acceptance and legitimacy from not only its chief rival Greece, but also the might of the Western European power players.

It's time for Turkey to face the truth. Turkey's real chances for future membership in the European Union, at least within the climate that Europe sits in at the current time and for the foreseeable future, is extremely limited.

First, Turkey is not "European", geographically or culturally. Turkey has around 95 percent of its land in Asia; of which the only benefit to the European Union would be control over the Strait of Bosporus, connecting the Mediterranean to the Black Sea. Perhaps, Russia could see this as an imminent threat by the European Union to infringe on Russian trade routes. Ethnic Turks migrated from what is now eastern Russia across central Asia to the Anatolian Peninsula. Yes, Turks are not truly "Arabic" peoples, which somewhat separates Turkey from other Middle Eastern nations. Turkey has a 98 percent Muslim majority, yet remains a secular nation. Although religious tolerance of minorities is practices, EU powers such as France and Germany can at times be leery of strong Christian sentiments. Promised referendums on Turkey's accession in France and Austria perhaps pose the largest threat to Turkey's candidacy.

Secondly, political and international relations pose a significant threat to Turkey's candidacy. Although Turkey would bring a large defense force into the EU, and act as a buffer state to turmoil in the Middle East, political challenges stand in the way. First, in the east, conflict with the Kurdish population must be resolved prior to accession. It may require Turkey to take a lead role in developing an independent, stable Kurdistan, to meet the wants from EU members. The situation in Cyprus also must be settled. Cyprus in claiming the entire island is the real "push-pin" of solving this crisis. Turkey will have to accept the loss of its claims in Northern Cyprus to gain Cypriot and further Greek acceptance. Although the eurocrisis strongly hurt Greek reputation, Greece remains a key player in the EU, and maintains a significant clout. Turkey-Greece relations would have to somehow find a benefit for working together before any significant support of Turkey's accession will be accepted by Greece. Turkey's relations with other non-EU states such as Armenia would also play a large role in acceptance by westerners. Yet, the only issue which binds Western Europe to Turkey is its loyal participation in NATO. Turkey is a necessary and strong ally in a hostile region.

Third, while Turkey's economic success continues to blossom, economic inequality remains a hot topic. Europe's consistent Keynesian economic policies might present somewhat of a shock to Turkey's powerful upper class. GDP per capita remains low, about half the EU average. Poor Turks would be willing to immigrate west, infiltrating nations hostile toward Islamic peoples. Poor Turks also would be willing to work at lower wages at the status quo, requiring Turkey to modernize significantly to catch up with European wage floors.

The accession of Turkey into the European Union is one that is very unlikely as the world sits today. Likewise, the prospect of a unique association of the EU with Turkey is one that would allow multiple benefits and avoid the long and tumultuous process of full accession. Turkey could perhaps become more of a provisional state to the EU in this regard. However, the ability of Turkey to gain internal and external acceptance for full accession is extremely unlikely today or in the near future.

ECONOMIC AND MILITARY INTEGRATION

A substantial squabbling point in the minds of European economists is the common currency of the European Union (EU), within the Eurozone, better known as the Euro.

As explained by Castleberry, Maniam, and Subramaniam, the Euro began as a unique idea to bring fairness to trade throughout the EU. The debate over the Euro began in 1998. Many people in dominant European economies opposed the Euro, laying claims that their economies would be drove backward; for example, German citizens opposed the Euro at a staggering seventy-one percent in 1998. Ironically, after the adoption of the Euro was slammed through by Berlin, the Euro's slight value decline immediately helped the German people and economy. Thus, beginning with the Euro's ribbon cutting in January 1999, the value shrunk compared to the strong United States dollar during the boom years of the Clinton era. Toward the modern history of the Euro, economic collapse paralyzed the western world, particularly striking the PIIGS (Portugal, Italy, Ireland, Greece, and Spain) with financial turmoil. Albeit, many nations like Greece and Spain were much worse than others economically, the Euro may have done the contrary to its original intention. The inability to maneuver a national currency by these nations created a waiting game and ultimately the reliance on EU aid. Additionally, the Euro is weakened by these debt crises, and instability of the European economy (Castleberry, Maniam, and Subramaniam[36]).

The European Central Bank (ECB) heads the operations for the Euro and the Eurozone.

---

[36] Castleberry, Douglas, Balasundram Maniam, and Geetha Subramaniam. "The Euro and the European Debt Crisis." *The International Business & Economics Research Journal (Online)* 13.1 (2014): 103,n/a. *ProQuest.* Web. 12 Aug. 2015.

According to europa.eu, the EU's official website, the ECB "implements economic and monetary policy", with their main goal of keeping prices stable, thus creating a solid economy. The powers of the ECB include, "monitoring foreign currency reserves, setting interest rates, loaning to commercial banks, supervising markets and institutions, authorizing production of banknotes, monitor price trends and price stability" and many more tasks. The governing council (decision-making), executive board (day to day execution), and general council (advisory and coordination), compose the ECB. Overall, the European System of Central Banks includes all 28 national banks from the member states, broken to the Eurosystem, of which is the cooperation of the Eurozone member central banks (europa.eu[37]).

---

[37] "European Central Bank (ECB)." *EUROPA*. European Union, n.d. Web. 12 Aug. 2015. <http://europa.eu/about-eu/institutions-bodies/ecb/index_en.htm>.

The Euro overall has had an adverse effect on Europe, of which works in both directions. Balcerowicz, et. al., provides a great insight into the state of the European economy. First off, the adoption of the Euro, according to Balcerowicz, et. al., Gross Domestic Product (GDP) per capita has remained level within the Eurozone in comparison to the United States, exemplifying that the Euro has maintained strong through the economic meltdown of the late 2000's decade. Also, since the adoption of the Euro, many member states have saw a vast acceleration in their economies as a result (Balcerowicz, et. al.[38]).

Although the Euro has been ridiculed by many, the outlook for some nations remains very strong. As displayed by Spoerry, Latvia is looking forward to some negative initial effects, but "a

---

[38] Balcerowicz, Lezeck, et. al. "Economic Growth in the European Union." *Lisbon Council E-Book* (2013): n. pag. Lisbon Council. Web. 12 Aug. 2015.

better bottom line". Latvia was considered likely to see the same transitionary effects as Estonia, a Baltic sister state. Since Latvia has sat in the European Exchange Rate Mechanism II (ERMII) and been linked to the Euro for a time now, the conversion is considerably easier than many other Euro newcomers. Latvian banks also see greater opportunity for lower interest rates (Spoerry[39])

Some nations, such as Italy, with a strong initial economy, has saw a hit as a result of Euro adoption. Balcerowicz, et. al., shows that Italian GDP per capita has fallen almost eight percentage points to the United States since 1999. Sweden, who joined the EU with a very poor economy in 1995, has vowed to not join the Euro. Since Sweden's accession in 1995, Swedish GDP per capita has gained thirteen percentage points on

[39] Spoerry, Lorenzo. "Experts See Positives for Latvian Banks in Euro Changeover." *SNL European Financials Daily* (2013) *ProQuest.* Web. 12 Aug. 2015.

the United States. During the rough stretch of economic turmoil between 2008 and 2013, the European Union overall GDP per capita change (-2.6 percent), remained higher than the Eurozone average (-3.5 percent), thanks to strong performance by non-Eurozone states such as Poland (+12.5 percent), Bulgaria (+3.6 percent), and Sweden (+3.4 percent). PIIGS members like Spain (-7.4 percent), Portugal (-7.5 percent), Italy (-9.0 percent), and Greece (-23.6 percent) display fault in the Eurosystem to keep GDP per capita level (Balcerowicz, et. al.[40]).

The European economy's complicated situation with multinational influences make it vulnerable to economic complications. Balcerowicz, et. al., best said that, "It is ultimately up to civil societies in the respective countries to fix the growth problems of their own countries"

---

[40] Balcerowicz, Lezeck, et. al. "Economic Growth in the European Union." *Lisbon Council E-Book* (2013): n. pag. Lisbon Council. Web. 12 Aug. 2015.

(Balcerowicz, et. al.[41]).   Europe's economic climate is tumultuous in being a loose union. Without complete economic integration or the collapse of the Euro, Europe's economy will be subjected to an inordinate amount of instability in the marketplace.

The European Union (EU) has a complex system of communal defense efforts waged by the member states. Yet, because they are managed as a part of the national military of member states, their allegiance to EU remains unclear. The possibility of an entirely, EU controlled security force or military force of the future remains unclear as well.   Albeit, EU defense policy is more rigidly set on security of the homeland (Europe) than their American allies.

---

[41] Balcerowicz, Lezeck, et. al. "Economic Growth in the European Union." *Lisbon Council E-Book* (2013): n. pag. Lisbon Council. Web. 12 Aug. 2015.

In response to the Kosovo War in the late 1990's, the European Union understood that they were in need of a rapid defense mechanism. Battlegroups became that reality. According to the European Council, the plan began use in 2003. Soon after initiatives by the "Big Three" (France, Germany, and United Kingdom) began in 2004 for a structure, which could be deployed at a full force of 1,500 personnel per group within 15 days. Battlegroups however, are made up by a single member state or a coalition of member states (European Council[42]). Battlegroups are at the forefront of the European Union's defense mechanism, and are driven by the "Big Three".

The partnership and obvious overlap of member states between the European Union and the North Atlantic Treaty Organization (NATO) also plays a large role in the European Union's

---

[42] European Council. "EU Battlegroups." (2009): n. pag. June 2009. Web. 14 Aug. 2015.

defense. Eichenberg displays that support for the European Union creating its own defense system very high, although this does not weaken NATO whatsoever. European citizens show that they want to have both NATO and European Security and Defense Policy. Dual members of NATO and the EU formulated compromise in 1996 (Eichenberg[43]). Dual cooperation between NATO and the European Union remains critical to EU defense policy, and as a result, obviously creates a stronger EU defense system with NATO alive and well.

As a result between defense cooperation and the overall development of a new European defense system, the "Big Three" of France, Germany, and the United Kingdom play a naturally large role in this development. At the

---

[43] Eichenberg, Richard C. "HAVING IT BOTH WAYS: EUROPEAN DEFENSE INTEGRATION AND THE COMMITMENT TO NATO." *Public opinion quarterly* 67.4 (2003): 627-59. *ProQuest.* Web. 14 Aug. 2015.

origin of this development, Grant claims that none of the three powers can make a significant reinforcement of EU defense without the support of the other two; whereas, France, Germany, and the United Kingdom must agree to make any action legitimate. Foreign policy of the United Kingdom often greatly opposes France's due to support and reserved attitudes towards American foreign policy respectively (Grant[44]). Mawdsley also agrees, pointing to the disagreement with the "Big Three" and their relationship with Iran. However, the "Big Three" have been able to make compromises, which further their cooperation in the European Security and Defense Policy (Mawdsley[45]). Just as benefit comes from the "Big Three" in being the largest contributors to EU

[44] Grant, Charles. "Europe's 'Big Three' must Steer the Union." *FT.com* (2003): 1. *ProQuest.* Web. 14 Aug. 2015.

[45] Mawdsley, Jocelyn. "The Arming of the European Union: Explaining the Armaments Dimension of European Security and Defence Policy." *Perspectives* 12.1 (2004): 7-21. *ProQuest.* Web. 14 Aug. 2015.

defense, their overall disagreements in a few vital areas result in a lack of leadership and commitment to foreign policy. Mawdsley further adds that because a large defense system has worked with the United States, it may not be quite as successful in the European Union. Yet, in Brussels, there remains little debate as military integration slowly continues (Mawsley[46]).

Denmark remains an interesting partner in EU defense. Historically as pointed to by Friis, Danes voted to oppose the Maastricht Treaty and voted against joining the Euro. Danish reservations show reluctance to join EU defense policy due to its lack of impact in the decision making process, dominated by the "Big Three"

---

[46] Mawdsley, Jocelyn. "The Arming of the European Union: Explaining the Armaments Dimension of European Security and Defence Policy." *Perspectives* 12.1 (2004): 7-21. *ProQuest.* Web. 14 Aug. 2015.

(Friis[47]). As a result, Lammers cites antagonism between Denmark and Germany historically. Although relations improved via NATO, Danes were "forced to bow to German interests" (Lammers[48]).

Although Denmark remains extremely reluctant to pursue greater integration with EU defense policy, it remains a strong partner in NATO. According to Ringsmose, Denmark's own defense has relied on strong NATO partnerships, particularly with Norway and the United States. As a result of the Cold War, Denmark and the other small European NATO members drifted into the wings of the United States. As a result Denmark's partnership is a comfortable one for

---

[47] Friis, Lykke. "The Battle Over Denmark: Denmark and the European Union." *Scandinavian Studies* 74.3 (2002): 379-96.*ProQuest.* Web. 14 Aug. 2015.

[48] Lammers, Karl Christian. "Living Next Door to Germany: Denmark and the German Problem." *Contemporary European History* 15.4 (2006): 453-72. *ProQuest.* Web. 14 Aug. 2015.

Denmark proper. Denmark sees America as being the key force in maintaining peace in Europe, particularly in defense against the Russian military juggernaut, but "also as a stabilizing force in European affairs" (Ringsmose[49]). Although NATO is not under European Union control it plays the largest role in historical and modern defense of EU member states. A strong NATO diminishes the need for a stronger EU defense force, and helps to deter any action against the increased military integration in Europe from the East.

Europe, and particularly Denmark, see the defense of Europe as a major issue. Alternatively, there is very little agreement on how that should be done within the EU proper. The reliance on

---

[49] Ringsmose, Jens. "Investing in Fighters and Alliances: Norway, Denmark, and the Bumpy Road to the Joint Strike Fighter."*International Journal* 68.1 (2013): 93-110. *ProQuest.* Web. 14 Aug. 2015.

national governments to provide for common defense of Europe remains logical, although the push for future integration remains imminent. The likelihood of significant agreement, especially within the "Big Three" on integrating defense policy seems very unlikely from the current standpoint. However, the communal defense of the European Union is one which cannot be ignored, and will drive EU member states to support one another at a time of crisis, of which can be provided for each other at the status quo, along with support from NATO, and other worldwide partners.

European Union (EU) security has been a topic that has broadened the power and reach of the EU proper since its beginning. With the modern development of many defense organizations, and deployment to conflicts in the Balkans and Africa, there remains one conflict that the EU has great concern over but has not taken significant action – Kosovo.

The newly independent state of Kosovo is an ethnic borderland of mainly Albanians between Albania proper and Serbia. As described by Bideleux, 90 percent of Kosovo's population is ethnically Albanian, with a small amount of Serbs in the north. Kosovo has been under indirect rule for decades stemming from the Ottoman oppression of Slavic Christians. As war broke out in 1912 between Serbia and Albania, Kosovo was ceded to Serbia in the peace deal. After the defense of Serbia against the Austro-Hungarians in the First World War, Yugoslavia was erected in 1931. The Italians rejoined Kosovo to Greater Albania during their occupation early in the Second World War. After the Germans fell to Yugoslavian nationalists in 1945, the assembly joined Kosovo to Serbia yet once again. Over the course of the next four decades leading to the Balkan Wars, Kosovo would continuously long for independence (Bideleux[50]).   As can be seen, Kosovo has been in many different struggles for centuries for independence, and its security and stability remains a major issue to today.

After the decades of strife, on 17 February 2008, Kosovo declared independence from Serbia. Bilefsky summarizes the event as being a difficult one for a new nation just a decade after a bloody civil war. The independence of Kosovo is disputed however; yet, many western nations recognized Kosovo's Independence. Since 1999, NATO has kept about 12,000 troops in Kosovo on peacekeeping missions.   The European Union sees this as an important security battle, sending in 1,800 police to keep peace inside of Kosovo. Kosovo's independence brings out much in the historical alliance between Russia and Serbia, as well as the separatist movements in other EU

[50] Bideleux, Robert. "Kosovo's Conflict." History Today 48.11 November 1998 (1998): n. pag. Kosovo's Conflict. *History Today,* 11 Sept. 1998. Web. 11 Aug. 2015.

member states. However Serbians within Kosovo remain vastly opposed to independence, and vow to maintain Serbian control (Bilefsky[51]).

European Union security forces have been ever present in the Balkan region since their inception. Missions in the Former Yugoslav Republic of Macedonia and Bosnia and Herzegovina have sparked vast controversy between the EU and Serbia. With EU and NATO forces committed to the peace and independence of Kosovo, an article from the Asia News Monitor, displays former United States Secretary of State Hillary Clinton claiming the EU brokered deal between Serbia and Kosovo that "There are no other realistic or better alternatives. And things will not get easier if difficult discussions are simply put off. This is good for Serbia. And it's good for Kosovo. It's good for your future and for

---

[51] Bilefsky, Dan. "Kosovo Declares Its Independence From Serbia." *New York Times* 18 Feb. 2008: n. pag. Print.

the everyday lives of the people in this region" (Asia News Monitor[52]).

European Union security forces although still remain in place. Although, it appears that the EU is having a difficulty in proving that further intervention in the Kosovo situation will bring more stability to the region. Struggles with Serbia continue to occur, particularly as Serbia strengthens military ties to the Russian juggernaut. Peace deals are saw by many to be the only method to ensure Balkan stability. The EU also remains hesitant to push as a unified force in the wake of anti-war riots involving many of the same member states in the NATO bombings of the late 1990's.

Stability in the Balkans remains a critical issue for not only NATO, but for the EU proper.

---

[52] "United States/European Union/Serbia/Kosovo: US, EU Push for Better Relations between Serbia and Kosovo." *Asia News Monitor* Oct 31 2012. *ProQuest.* Web. 11 Aug. 2015.

In a region of constant ethnic conflict for centuries, it remains a critical stability zone between western and Russian influences. Likewise, European security forces will be required to maintain peaceful security for the Balkans to provide for future expansion or integration within the region. Although the EU defense forces could overwhelm Serbian presence, it remains critical to maintain political cohesiveness in the region, both for Kosovo's people, and the sake of west-east relations in Europe.

CONCLUDING REMARKS

The most important thing is not really plain content, but it is more a theory that riding the middle almost never works. I have discovered that the EU's plan of riding the middle when it comes to further integration rarely ever worked. Subsequently, it required a true analysis to see which side of that bubble was the correct side to choose – integration or devolution.

For instance, the legislative and judicial process' ride a fine line in distributing power between national and EU governance. The European Court of justice rightfully had to take control over supremacy of laws, directly bringing the entire EU under their rule and taking the EU off of the bubble firmly toward integration.

Talk about the Euro is widely seen as a good thing by the wealthy and a bad thing by the ordinary people in Europe. Euro adopting nations have fared poorly, particularly against non-Euro EU states like Poland and Sweden. Perhaps here the Euro truly does not work.

Defense policy is something that many nations don't want to give up control over. Member states recognize a need for common defense, but many who are NATO members see NATO as a more reasonable partner for defense, such as Denmark's situation. Additionally, many EU members see the United States in two different lights. France for example has an antagonistic look at the US and UK in their somewhat interlinked foreign policy. Meanwhile, strong NATO allies, and EU devolutionary members like Denmark and the UK see the United States as an integral part of European stability and security against the East. While, common defense is a good thing for EU member states, it may not be an item that the EU is adapted to tackle.

Ultimately, the middle road might be the ultimate decision. But with small pieces to the big puzzle it is critical to take a firm stance, particularly in government, and make sure that that stance is in the right direction.